A BETTER G SWING

By Damien Hosking

Dedicated To

My Dad

TABLE OF CONTENTS

INTRODUCTION

Golf has always been a noble sport where golfers often help their direct competitors. It is almost like the golfer wants a proper challenge - with his competitor to be at the top of his game.

This empathy and sportsmanship means competitors often help each other with tips, swing theories, and advice.

Tips like "keep your head down" and "swing straight back and straight through" have been handed down from generation to generation of golfers.

However, just because some information has been around for a long time, doesn't necessarily make it effective. A lot of this advice is completely wrong, and can damage your swing and possibly your entire game.

Hi, my name is Damien and I have been involved within the golf industry for more than 35 years (but who's counting!). During those years I have been a competitive player, caddy, a golf retailer, driving range owner and coach.

Each day at my driving range I would see pupils and customers practicing and trying to implement different golfing tips and pieces of advice to in an effort to improve their golf swing.

Occasionally, these golfers would have success in the short term; however after a while the tip seemed to "wear off" and the original problem would come back.

This book will reveal 30 of the most destructive golfing tips. You will learn why these tips were given, what problems they will cause, and an alternative solution that will improve your game.

At the end of each tip the acronym of K.I.S.S is presented. (**Keep it simple stupid**). Choose one or two of these simplified reminders as a quick cue while playing or practicing.

Enjoy.

1 THE TIP: KEEP YOUR HEAD DOWN.

WHY IS THIS TIP GIVEN?

It takes precision to hit a ball consistently to a target 250 yards or more away.

It is theorized that keeping your head down will reduce body movement and therefore increase precision.

THE PROBLEM WITH IMPLEMENTING THE TIP.

Any good golf swing requires power and precision. To achieve any amount of power, large muscles like the back, shoulders, chest and legs must be used.

The backswing motion must be made with a turning of the shoulders so that at the top of the backswing your back is pointing in the direction of the target (a turn of around 90 degree).

Conversely, on the downswing, your shoulders should unwind so that on completion of the swing your chest will be facing the target (a shoulder unwind of 180 degree from where they were at the top).

If you keep your head down throughout the swing, the big muscle movement described above will not be possible and you may injure your neck.

At the very least you will be swinging in a very constricted manner.

Your arms will be forced to provide most of the power, which will lead to many other issues.

A BETTER GOLF SWING

While your shoulders are coiling up on the backswing (turning your back to face the target) allow your head to naturally swivel so that your chin has turned slightly to the right.

Keep your eye on the ball, but seeing the ball out of the corner of the left eye is enough. You do not need to stare directly down at the ball during your swing.

On the forward swing, unwind your shoulders and face your chest to the target. Allow your head to turn to the left and look square on to the target.

The real key to consistent ball striking is to *maintain the posture that you created at address throughout the entire swing.*

Assuming you have taken a fairly normal address position, your upper body (the spine) will be tilted towards the ball. On the backswing you need to rotate your shoulders around this spine angle.

If your upper body pulls away from the ball at the top of the backswing, the posture established at address would be compromised.

The same applies on the downsizing. If your back is straightening as the club is coming down, your chest will be further from the ball.

This will cause topped shots and other problems. Your head will be "up" if your spine is straightening at anytime throughout the swing, however, lifting your head is only a symptom of losing your posture.

Attempting to keep your head down will not solve the actual problem.

Learn to maintain your spine angle and allow natural head movement for a more powerful and consistent strike.

K.I.S.S.

Stay in the shot - cover the ball with your chest - maintain your spine angle - allow your head to rotate naturally.

2 THE TIP: KEEP YOUR LEFT ARM STRAIGHT

WHY IS THIS TIP GIVEN?

In the same way that a spoke of a bicycle wheel forms an unbroken radius within the wheel, it is thought that the left arm must stay straight to maintain the swings radius and maximize the power and width of the swing.

THE PROBLEM WITH IMPLEMENTING THE TIP

Tension throughout a golf swing is very destructive. The vast majority of golfers do indeed attempt to keep the left arm straight while fully coiling the shoulders.

This "straight left arm" adds an enormous amount of strain and force to the neck, upper back and even the shoulder joint.

A BETTER GOLF SWING

Instead of thinking about keeping the left arm straight on the back swing, concentrate on what the right arm is doing.

At the top of the backswing, make sure that your right elbow bends at no more than a 90-degree angle.

At the top of the backswing (when you maintain a 90 –degree angle at the right elbow) there will be a large gap formed in between your hands and rear shoulder. This gap is how you create the width of swing that maximizes power.

At this point (the top of the backswing) your left arm should feel soft and relaxed. You do not need to have the left elbow locked. The left elbow should have a slight flex and natural amount of "give" to it.

Arriving at the top of the backswing in this position will give you plenty of distance producing width, while at the same time keeping any tension and strain at a minimum.

K.I.S.S

Soft elbows - produce a gap at the top -90 degree bend in the right arm.

3 THE TIP: SWING THE CLUB STRAIGHT BACK AND STRAIGHT THROUGH.

WHY IS THIS TIP GIVEN?

Hitting the ball straight is a goal for almost all golfers. Many players (and coaches) see the golf swing as a series of straight lines.

One might think that swinging the club head through on a straight line would also make the ball fly in a straight line.

THE PROBLEM WITH IMPLEMENTING THE TIP

The design of any golf club dictates that the golfer stands to the side of the ball while taking the address position.

As the upper body coils on the backswing, it is impossible to keep the club head travelling on a straight line away from the ball. The only way to do so is to unnaturally push the club back away from the ball by separating your arms from your body.

Any time you separate the arms from the big muscles of the torso you lose power, and a consistent strike will require a lot more timing and/ or practice.

A BETTER GOLF SWING

Once you have taken your normal address position, (standing to the inside of the ball) imagine that the grip end of the club (referred to as the butt of the club) is attached to your body somewhere around the belt buckle.

As you start your backswing, keep imagining that the club is still attached to your body. Notice how the club head is curving *in* on a natural arc. The club head is definitely not moving straight back artificially.

Continue with the feeling that the club is connected to your body until your hands have reached about hip high and the club shaft is parallel to the ground. Only now should your arms and club start to lift away from the turning of the body.

Because the club head started its journey on the correct arc, it will have a much better chance of staying on the correct arc throughout the rest of the swing.

The forward swing is virtually a mirror image of the backswing in the sense that once the ball has been struck, the club head will again swing on an arc back to the inside - never straight through.

K.I.S.S

Low and around – imagine the butt of the club connected to the turning of your body.

4 THE TIP: MAKE SURE YOUR DIVOTS POINT TOWARDS THE TARGET.

WHY IS THIS TIP GIVEN?

It is said that a divot pointing at the target is evidence that the club head was travelling exactly down the target line through impact.

THE PROBLEM WITH IMPLEMENTING THE TIP

If you were successful in having the divot point at the target, the ball will fly to the right and miss the target. Since the club must travel on an arc (see tip 3) to hit the ball *at* the target, the divot must point slightly *left* of the target.

If you hit the ball first and then take the divot, the club head will be travelling on the inside arc (while taking the divot) and moving to the left of the target. Again, by having a club head path that (incorrectly) produces divots *pointing at the target*, the ball will fly to the right of the target.

A BETTER GOLF SWING

Assuming you have taken a square stance, as in tip 3, the only way to have your divots point at the target is to artificially swing the club head "down the line".

To achieve this you would need to separate the arms from the turning of the body through impact. Instead, try to get the feeling that your upper arms are staying very close to your chest through impact.

The inside of your upper left arm must remain connected to your rib cage until half way into the follow through. After this halfway point you can release the arms away from the body into a free flowing follow through.

Keeping the arms connected to the turning of the body through impact will have the club head correctly swinging to the inside. This will have the divots pointing slightly left of the target and the ball flying *at* the target.

K.I.S.S

Stay connected - fold the left arm through impact - swing the club on the inside during the follow through.

5 THE TIP: BEND YOUR KNEES

WHY IS THIS TIP GIVEN?

With the ball sitting on the ground or a tee, it is necessary to have the club head coming in low to the ground. You want your irons actually striking the ground and producing divots aligned slightly left of the target (see tip 4).

Players are told to bend their knees in an effort to lower the body and club head throughout the swing.

THE PROBLEM WITH IMPLEMENTING THE TIP

The first problem is that players receiving this advice will bend their knees way too much.

Once the knees have been bent too much at address, there is nowhere else for them to go but to straighten up during the backswing.

This straightening of the knees inevitably causes the upper body to also straighten and cause inconsistencies.

A BETTER GOLF SWING

In taking your address position momentarily keep the knees dead straight. Bend over from the hips until the club head touches the ground. Now simply *unlock* your knees.

Having the knees in the "off lock" or "soft" position at address will allow the legs and hips to make an uninhibited backswing.

The correct time to have the knees bending is during the downswing.

Once the top of the backswing has been reached (and the knees have stayed "off lock"), a lot of good golfers will initiate the downswing with a lower body "squatting action".

This squatting action braces the body for the strike and has the knees more bent than the "off lock" position of the backswing.

Once the ball has been struck, the knees should return to the off lock position to allow the upper body to freely unwind into a complete follow through.

K.I.S.S

Flex your knees going back - squat down coming through - knees off lock

6 THE TIP: HAVE SQUARE SHOULDERS AT IMPACT

WHY IS THIS TIP GIVEN?

A club head that is pointing down the target line at moment of impact maximizes the chances of hitting a straight shot.

We are told to have our shoulders square at impact so that the club path is related to our shoulder alignment.

THE PROBLEM WITH IMPLEMENTING THE TIP

As you make your backswing your left arm will steadily rise up and across your chest.

To maintain the power that you build up on the backswing, your arms and club must lag behind the unwinding of your legs and torso coming down.

On the downswing your left arm needs to stay up across your chest as your torso unwinds. By the time your arms and hands are in the position to hit the ball, your shoulders will be open and pointing slightly left of the target.

If a golfer achieves square shoulders at impact, the arms will have no other option than to come down the chest way too early, resulting in a "blocked" arm position. This will cause a big loss of power and a faulty club path.

A BETTER GOLF SWING

Instead of having your shoulders square at impact, concentrate on having your *forearms* square at impact.

If your forearms are square at impact (an arrow laying on top of both the forearms would point at the target) and the arms slightly behind the torso, the shoulders will be pointing left of the target.

This will have the club head briefly travelling down the target line at the moment of impact.

You will have maintained all the stored up energy and power of the backswing, and will be hitting the ball fairly straight, as directed by the club head and forearm positioning.

K.I.S.S

Square forearms - open shoulders.

7 THE TIP: PAUSE AT THE TOP OF THE BACKSWING.

WHY IS THIS TIP GIVEN?

A common complaint from many golfers is that they start their downswing before they reach the top of their backswing.

A pause at the top is suggested to break the backswing up from the forward swing.

THE PROBLEM WITH IMPLEMENTING THE TIP

Many golfers hearing this tip will do such a good job of pausing at the top of their backswing that some parts of their body will actually come to a complete stop.

Stopping any part of the body at the top ruins momentum and timing of the forward swing.

A BETTER GOLF SWING

A slight pause at the top of the backswing isn't a bad thing as long as it is the club, and not your body, that is pausing. During the backswing your hips will achieve their full turn before the shoulders are coiled. At the moment that your hips start to unwind towards the target, your shoulders still have a little more winding up to do.

Because your upper and lower body will be moving in two different directions simultaneously, the club will appear to pause or "hover" at the top of the backswing.

As long as it is only your club that is pausing, your rhythm and timing will be just fine.

K.I.S.S

Hover the club head at the top of the backswing - feel the weight of the club head at the top.

8 THE TIP: SWING AROUND A CENTERED PIVOT POINT

WHY IS THIS TIP GIVEN?

To keep the body motion to a minimum and give us more precision, we are told to swing around one pivot point which is located directly through the centre of our neck and chest.

THE PROBLEM WITH IMPLEMENTING THE TIP

The most common mistake that is made when a player attempts to swing around one centered axis point is the "reverse pivot".

As the player is trying to swing centered on the backswing, the majority of the body weight inevitably pushes to the front foot. At the top of the backswing, the body will be leaning towards the target with weight on the front foot.

On the downswing the weight has nowhere else to go except to the rear foot and an unbalanced fall back follow through is produced.

A BETTER GOLF SWING

At address, imagine two lines running straight up from your feet to your shoulders.

These lines represent your *two pivot points*. On the backswing you should be coiling your shoulders and allowing the body weight to move to the inside of your back foot.

The forward swing will be this but in reverse. Unwind your shoulders and hips and allow the majority of your weight to transfer to the second pivot point - the inside of the front foot.

Doing this allows you to have a full weight transfer and free flowing swing.

K.I.S.S

Shoulders coil to the inside of the back foot - shoulders uncoil over the inside of the front foot.

9 THE TIP: KEEP YOUR HEAD LEVEL (ALSO STATED AS MAINTAIN YOUR HEIGHT)

WHY IS THIS TIP GIVEN?

A preoccupation with trying to keep the body still throughout the swing is the motivation for this tip.

THE PROBLEM WITH IMPLEMENTING THE TIP

To achieve a free flowing swing, the hips must be allowed to move uninhibited.

Your knees need to move in a way that allows this uninhibited movement. With the head remaining level throughout the swing, the knees and hips are unable to do their job effectively.

This limits the amount of desirable compression (lowering) that the upper body makes on the backswing.

A BETTER GOLF SWING.

On the backswing, your right knee is a great focal point.

As you wind up your shoulders on the backswing, maintain the flex in your right knee (remember tip 5 - do not *bend* your knees). As your hips are turning in the backswing, allow the flexed right knee to move backwards a couple of inches from its original starting position.

Because of the turning hips and the retracted right knee, the right glute muscle will stick out further behind you.

This is a very coiled, loaded and dynamic position to achieve. The only way to be in this position is by allowing your head to lower through the backswing, which puts you in a more compressed position.

Your body will be working somewhat like a car jack, (as your head lowers your butt pushes back and out).

At the top of your backswing your hips and butt will be in a very "deep" position. This creates a lot of space between your body and the ball and gives you plenty of room to swing the arms into on the downswing.

With your head lowering, deep hips, and space created to swing your arms into on the downswing, a higher level of consistent ball striking will be achieved.

K.I.S.S

Compress into the ground - create space - deep hips – allow your head to lower.

10 THE TIP: RESTRICT THE HIPS FROM TURNING ON THE BACKSWING TO CREATE X FACTOR

WHY IS THIS TIP GIVEN?

At the top of the backswing, if an imaginary line was drawn across the shoulders and another line was drawn across the hips, the differential between these lines would be referred to as the x factor.

We are told that the x factor (and therefore power) will increase by retarding the hip turn on the backswing while coiling the shoulders as far as possible.

THE PROBLEM WITH IMPLEMENTING THE TIP.

First of all, achieving a big shoulder turn while restricting the hips is physically very taxing.

Even if you create a large backswing differential between the shoulders and the hips, it does not guarantee that the differential will be maintained into the forward swing.

All you have done is unnecessarily stressed and strained your lumbar spine for potentially no good reason.

A BETTER GOLF SWING

Instead of creating x factor on the backswing, create x factor on the forward swing.

At the beginning of the downswing you will need to simultaneously transfer your weight to your front foot, open your hips up *and* keep the shoulders in the top of the backswing position for as long as possible.

A stretch is produced within the upper and lower body, creating x factor through the swing at the appropriate time.

It will still take some physical effort to have x factor on the downswing, however any torsion and power created at this point will have a much greater chance of being delivered to the ball at moment of impact.

K.I.S.S

Open hips – hold your shoulders back – feel that you are keeping the arms in the top of the backswing position for as long as you can.

11 THE TIP: ROLL YOUR WRISTS TO SQUARE THE CLUBFACE.

WHY IS THIS TIP GIVEN?

The slice, which is a ball curving off severely in flight from left to right (for the right hander), is one of the most common shots in golf.

As soon as a player hits the dreaded slice he is told to roll the right hand over the left hand on the downswing, closing the club face and hopefully preventing a slice.

THE PROBLEM WITH IMPLEMENTING THE TIP.

At the moment of impact a club head can reach speeds of between 70 and 100mph. To use the hands to square the club face requires too much timing and practice for the average golfer.

You will be fighting a never-ending battle of not enough wrist roll (slice) and too much wrist roll (hook).

A BETTER GOLF SWING

A much easier way to create a consistently straight ball flight, is to link the squaring of the club face with the turning of the body through impact.

At the midpoint of the downswing, your hips will be square to the target with your belt buckle pointing at the ball.

At the same time that your body is in this position, the clubface will be "side on" and at a 90 degree open position relative to the ball.

As the downswing progresses and the body is turning left through impact, *the entire left arm needs to be rotating counter clockwise.* This causes the clubface to go from the side on position (90 degree open) to being square (club face pointing at the target) at moment of impact.

The turning of the hips will be pulling the torso around to the target while the entire left arm is rotating left, which will in turn square the clubface at the moment of impact.

To be squaring the club with the turning of the body is a more reliable and consistent way, as compared to rolling of the wrists and the use of the hands to control the squaring of the club face.

K.I.S.S

Turn through impact - link the entire left arm with the turning of the body.

12 THE TIP: HIT YOUR PUTTS WITH TOPSPIN.

WHY IS THIS TIP GIVEN?

A ball rolling towards the hole on the putting surface rolls with topspin.

We are told to hit the ball with topspin so the ball will hug the putting green and roll smoothly towards the hole.

THE PROBLEM WITH IMPLEMENTING THE TIP

Trying to hit a putt with topspin will have the player hitting the ball in an unnaturally upward motion.

The design of any putter has the blade being very shallow compared to your other clubs. If you try to hit up on the ball, you run the risk of hitting the ball too low on the clubface and missing the sweet spot, which can make judging distance difficult.

A BETTER GOLF SWING (A BETTER PUTT)

High-speed video analysis tells us that all putts initially start their journey with backspin.

Due to the shallowness of any putter blade, the sole of the club needs to be very close to the ground in order to hit the center of the ball in the middle of the club face.

Striking the ball with a *forward pushing motion*, while concentrating on having the club head moving *level with the ground*, is a much better option and leads to better distance control.

K.I.S.S

Push the ball to the hole - keep the putter head low.

13 THE TIP: SWING IN TO OUT TO STOP SLICING

WHY IS THIS TIP GIVEN?

When a golfer slices the ball to the right of the target, many golfers will say that the club head must be travelling drastically to the left of the target and cutting across the ball - producing clockwise side spin.

To combat the side spin we are told to swing the club more from behind our bodies (in) to a position where the club is moving to the right of the target (out).

This in-to-out swing path is meant to stop the club from cutting across the ball and therefore stop the slice.

THE PROBLEM WITH IMPLEMENTING THE TIP

The initial and most destructive cause of the slice is the open club face at the moment of impact.

The open clubface deludes the golfer into feeling that he has to compensate and swing to the left of the target. This has the ball starting left and then curving right.

However, when the player swings in to out (*before fixing the open clubface*), the ball will be struck so far to the right that after hitting a few shots like this his instincts kick in and he starts swinging to the left again.

A BETTER GOLF SWING

The starting point to fix a slice (or hook for that matter) is to fix the club face alignment at impact.

Only when the club face returns to square at impact should the club path be looked at.

There are many reasons as to why the club face may be open at impact. Generally, any club face that is open on the backswing and early on in the downswing will be open at impact.

Look for the reason as to why the club face is open on the backswing. Once you have found and corrected the cause of the open clubface, you can experiment with swinging in-to-out.

Dealing with the club face first and having it return to square at impact will stop most of the clockwise side spin action on the ball.

With the club face returning to square at impact, you won't feel the need to start the ball left of the target, and you will be able to swing the club down on a much better path.

K.I.S.S

Close club face first - then swing in to out.

14 THE TIP: POINT THE CLUB SHAFT DOWN THE LINE AT THE TOP.

WHY IS THIS TIP GIVEN?

It is said that having the club shaft parallel to the target line at the top of the backswing makes it easier to swing the club down on a path that is parallel to the target line.

THE PROBLEM WITH IMPLEMENTING THE TIP

The first move from backswing to downswing (transition) is possibly the most critical phase of the entire swing.

If the club shaft is not on the correct path on the downswing by the time your left arm is parallel to the ground, you will need to compensate in some way to be in better hitting position.

The best position to have the club in at the midpoint on the downswing (when the left arm is parallel to the ground) is with the butt end of the club pointing directly at the ball/target line.

If you have the club pointing down the line at the top of the backswing, the only way to be on plane during the downswing midpoint position is to make a flattening or "layback" movement of the club shaft.

If there is no flattening, the club will be coming into the hitting zone too steep. This will force a compensatory move.

A BETTER GOLF SWING.

To completely avoid the need to flatten or "lay back" the club through the transition phase of the swing, *point the club shaft slightly left of the target* at the top of the backswing.

Modern players on tour prefer to have the club point left of the target at the top of the back swing.

This position is sometimes incorrectly called "laid off". If the club shaft is only slightly left of the target at the top, it could be referred to as being "on line" (or even on plane). The term "laid off" should only apply to a club shaft that points drastically left of target at the top.

When you swing your arms down from the "on line" club position (club pointing slightly left), the club will automatically be on plane at the mid point, making any manipulations and flattening of the club totally unnecessary.

To avoid the need to re rout the club coming down, have the club shaft point slightly left of the target at the top of the backswing.

K.I.S.S

Point the club slightly left at the top.

15 THE TIP: SWING THE CLUB TO PARALLEL ON THE BACKSWING.

WHY IS THIS TIP GIVEN?

To achieve the "correct" length of backswing at the top, we are told the club should be parallel to the ground.

This parallel position is often viewed to be the perfect length of backswing for all full shots.

THE PROBLEM WITH IMPLEMENTING THE TIP

This arbitrary parallel position does not take into account a golfer's flexibility, strength or even age.

If a player happens to be flexible enough to swing the club past parallel, then swinging short of parallel will represent an under swing for this particular golfer. If you are physically unable to get the club back to parallel, but somehow achieve a parallel position (usually by drastically bending your arms at the top), you will have over swung relative to your own natural length of swing.

Both of these scenarios will negatively affect your rhythm and timing.

A BETTER GOLF SWING.

Every golfer has a perfect backswing length for full shots.

If you achieve a coiled shoulder turn, have your right elbow bent no more than 90 degree (see tip 2), and maintain a solid grip on the club, your natural backswing will be the right length.

This might mean that the club is short of parallel, or indeed past parallel. As long as you are swinging to a length of backswing that is not forced – or unnaturally restricted, you will have achieved a backswing length that is right for your body. Your rhythm and timing will improve because your body has reached its own natural length of backswing.

K.I.S.S

Coil back a natural amount.

16 THE TIP: DROP THE HANDS STRAIGHT DOWN FROM THE TOP

WHY IS THIS TIP GIVEN?

We are told to drop the hands straight down into the "slot".

This is done to stop the hands and club shaft from swinging over on the downswing, coming from outside the target line and hitting a pull shot to the left.

THE PROBLEM WITH IMPLEMENTING THE TIP

Coming too far to the inside of the ball is just as bad as coming too far from the outside of the ball. When you drop your hands and club straight down from the top, there is too much vertical movement and not enough horizontal movement of the club.

Once the club is dropped down vertically it will approach the ball from behind the player's body in what would be considered a stuck position. As a compensation move, the player then thrusts the club in a horizontal movement towards the ball, (since the horizontal movement has to make up for the vertical movement at some point).

This horizontal thrusting causes the upper body to lift up and pull back and away from the ball.

This type of swing takes many hours of dedicated practice to control.

A BETTER GOLF SWING

There is a perfect slot to swing the club into on the downswing.

From the top of your backswing, aim to bring your hands back down into the same position that they occupied at address.

If you stand behind and watch a good player starting the downswing, you will see their hands and club shaft move in a *diagonal direction* back towards the original hand position.

At the top of your backswing, imagine a diagonal line from the butt of the club through to where your hand position was at address and all the way into the ground. The end of this imaginary diagonal line will be somewhere between the toes and the ball.

When bringing your arms down from the top, try to have the butt of the club travel down this diagonal line. Not too much vertical, not too much horizontal.

This diagonal path from the top of the swing is the most uncomplicated way to bring the club down into a consistent hitting plane.

K.I.S.S

Hands to hands - diagonally down.

17 THE TIP: POINT THE CLUB DOWN THE TOE LINE HALF WAY INTO THE FOLLOW THROUGH.

WHY IS THE TIP GIVEN?

There are usually two bits of advice given at once with this tip.

We are told to throw our arms away from the body and to point the club shaft straight down the toe/target line halfway into the follow through.

Supposedly the club head speed will be maximized due to the throwing of the arms while the path of the club will be down the line for accuracy.

THE PROBLEM WITH IMPLEMENTING THIS TIP

As stated before, anytime you move your arms out and away from your source of strength (your torso), the swings power, timing and consistency will suffer.

Swinging the club like this during the follow through is sometimes called a "chase release". When you see someone doing this, it looks like the club head chases down the toe line after the ball.

However, the chance of consistently hitting the ball long and straight with the chase release pattern is very small.

A BETTER GOLF SWING

Instead of pointing the club shaft down the toe/target line half way into the follow through, have the club shaft point down your heel/target line.

To do this, you need to keep your left arm close and connected to the left side of your body as you turn through impact. To help achieve this, the left elbow should be allowed to fold into the body after impact.

Once you reach the halfway point of the follow through in this position, the club shaft will still be pointing directly at the target, however, the club will be down the heel/target line.

This shows that the club was correctly swinging on the inside arc with your divots pointing slightly left of the target (tip 4). It also shows that the arms and body turned through impact in unison.

You will still be able to generate plenty of club head speed since your arms will be connected to your power source and the turning your body will whip the club head through impact.

K.I.S.S

Fold the left arm through impact - Keep arms connected to the body through the hitting area.

18 THE TIP: ACCELERATE THE PUTTER THROUGH IMPACT.

WHY IS THE TIP GIVEN?

If the ball is struck with a decelerating blow and the putter head slows down as the ball is hit, the ball will roll tentatively afterwards.

Any imperfections or borrow on the putting surface will be magnified and the ball will likely roll off the intended line.

We are therefore told that a positive stroke that "accelerates through impact" is better.

THE PROBLEM WITH IMPLEMENTING THE TIP

When a player attempts to accelerates the putter head close to impact, the hands have a tendency to cause a jerky and uncontrolled stroke.

A BETTER GOLF SWING (A BETTER PUTT)

The club head should be accelerating through impact, but gravity and inertia, not the hands, need to supply that acceleration.

A good comparison is imagining a child on a swing. As the child swings down there is a steady and increasing speed generated by the forces of gravity, with the downward moving force pushing the child through the swing arc.

You should feel the putter head steadily increasing speed at the exact moment that it starts its downswing.

This acceleration needs to come from gravity and momentum, and not any part of your body.

K.I.S.S

Let gravity and momentum accelerate the club head.

19 THE TIP: OPEN YOUR STANCE FOR PITCHING AND CHIPPING

WHY IS THIS TIP GIVEN?

An open stance is achieved for short shots when the hips, knees and feet are all pointing well left of the target and "out of the way".

This supposedly gives us room to bring our arms and club through impact.

THE PROBLEM WITH IMPLEMENTING THE TIP

With the feet, knees and hips all pointing well left of the target, the tendency will be to swing the club along the line of the lower body and cut across the ball.

This is a great strategy if you are looking to lob the ball high or get out of a bunker.

But if you are playing a standard pitch or chip, the swing path needs to be aligned towards the target to achieve a uniform height and roll on the ball.

A BETTER GOLF SWING (A BETTER PITCH)

Maintaining the lower body square to the target line while at the same time having clearance through the lower body, is the key to a good short game.

Take your stance with the lower body perfectly square to the intended line of flight. Now turn both feet 45 degrees to the left. At this point, both of your feet are pointing left of the target and appear very open. Now pull your right leg and foot back a few inches.

What we are trying to do is to have the angle of your feet pointing left of the target while at the same having your toes touching an imaginary line that would be square to the target. Pulling your right leg back a few inches will facilitate this. Also, allow both of your thighs to rotate left on their axis.

Taking this kind of stance gives you the *sensation* that your entire lower body is open to the target which creates a *feeling of space* to swing the arms and club into.

Since your lower body is actually still square to the target line, you will be able to swing your club through and see the target line much easier.

K.I.S.S

Keep a squarely open stance.

20 THE TIP: SUPINATE THE LEFT HAND AT IMPACT

WHY IS THE TIP GIVEN?

At impact, a supinated left hand is achieved when the back of the left hand is turning down to face the ground with the entire left hand in front of the ball.

Hitting the ball with a downward compression strike (particularly irons) works well.

Having the back of the left hand in front of the ball while working the back of the hand down to face the ground will help you accomplish this.

THE PROBLEM WITH IMPLEMENTING THE TIP

The golf swing is a series of chain reactions.

When a player tries to supinate *without* having the other swing elements in place, the hands are *forced* into a supinated position.

A BETTER GOLF SWING.

There is no need to physically supinate the left hand through impact.

A good golf swing will ensure that at moment of impact, the left hand will be leading the club head.

If the hips and upper body stop unwinding, the arms and hands will be cast into the ball too early. This will cause the back of the left hand to cup (pronate), which is the opposite of supination.

At the start of your downswing, focus on the turning and unwinding of the body.

The weight is to be transferring to the left pivot point (see tip 8), which will keep the arms correctly behind the body and cause a pulling effect on the club.

As you swing down into the hitting zone, continue to unwind the hips and upper body. This body movement will apply the necessary forces to the arms and club which will cause the back of the left hand to be in front of the ball, and working down as you strike.

It is because of these body movements and physics that you don't need to think about supination.

K.I.S.S

Transfer the weight left - allow the arms and club to lag slightly.

21 THE TIP: DO NOT LET THE LEFT HEEL RISE OFF THE GROUND DURING THE BACKSWING

WHY IS THIS TIP GIVEN?

To build torsion for more power, you should minimize the hip turn on the backswing.

Keeping the left heel down will reduce the amount of turn that the hips are able to produce. With the left heel "planted" during the backswing, the tendency to "stand up" on the backswing will be eliminated.

These two ideas combine into a popular, yet incorrect, golfing tip.

THE PROBLEM WITH IMPLEMENTING THE TIP

For the vast majority of golfers, less hip turn means less shoulder turn and amount of available power.

A BETTER GOLF SWING

Concentrate instead on allowing the left knee to *fold* behind the ball while rolling the left ankle in towards the ball (as compared to keeping the left foot "planted" on the ground).

There will be enough hip turn and shoulder coil with the left knee and ankle *folding in.*

In order to achieve the power of the original tip, you need to work on your x factor *on the downswing* (refer to tip 10).

With the correct folding action of the left heel, ankle and knee, (and x factor being produced on the forward swing), you will have more than enough power.

K.I.S.S

Fold the knee behind the ball - x factor forward swing.

22 THE TIP: INCREASE CLUB HEAD SPEED FOR GREATER DISTANCE

WHY IS THIS TIP GIVEN?

Greater club head speed leads to greater distance.

Nowadays, distance (particularly off the tee) is a pre-requisite for top line golf; therefore people are always looking for ways to increase their club head speed for greater distance.

THE PROBLEM WITH IMPLEMENTING THIS TIP:

When players try to increase the speed of the club head, their entire swing speeds up and causes a loss of balance, rhythm, and timing.

A BETTER GOLF SWING.

The easiest way to achieve consistent distance is to forget about increasing club head speed and concentrate on hitting the sweet spot (or centre) of the club head.

When the ball strikes the dead centre of the clubface, the mass and energy of the club head is transferred to the ball.

When striking the sweet spot, ball speed, trajectory and accuracy are all enhanced.

This way, maximum distance is achieved without any unnecessary energy being expelled by attempting to swing the club head faster and faster.

K.I.S.S

Hit the sweet spot - swing the club head through an imaginary gate during the impact zone.

23 THE TIP: USE A HIGH COMPRESSION GOLF BALL FOR ADDED DISTANCE

WHY IS THIS TIP GIVEN?

A high compression golf ball will "react" or bounce off of the club head faster.

We've all seen a player bouncing two golf balls on a hard surface and choosing the ball to play with that bounces the highest.

THE PROBLEM WITH IMPLEMENTING THE TIP

Unfortunately, if you are using a high compression golf ball (for more distance) but have an average or slower swing speed, you will not be able to "squash" the golf ball against the club face.

The potential energy of the club head will *not* be transferred to the ball and you will actually *lose distance.*

A BETTER GOLF SWING

A golf ball that is matched to a golfers swing speed ensures that it will be squashed at impact, and the amount of energy that is available gets transferred to the ball.

To find a ball that matches your swing speed, your local pro can measure your club head speed and recommend a ball that is compatible with your individual speed.

K.I.S.S

Learn to hit the centre of the club face for more distance - Experiment with different balls - speak with your pro.

24 THE TIP: USE STIFF SHAFTED CLUBS TO STOP SLICING

WHY IS THIS TIP GIVEN?

A club shaft that is "soft" or flexible tends to be associated with a large amount of curve on the ball.

It is suggested that a stiff shafted club will "keep the club head more stable" through impact.

THE PROBLEM WITH IMPLEMENTING THE TIP

All shafts have a certain amount of flex and kick point.

The club shaft is the most dynamic and important part of a golf club. As your downswing progresses, the shaft will "bend" at the moment of impact with a certain amount of "bowing" of the club. (Look at any high-speed video of a top player at impact to see how much bowing there actually is).

The kick point is responsible for the bowing, which helps square the club face.

If you are already hitting a big slice and opt for stiff shafts, the shaft won't flex and bow and help you square the club face at impact.

The slice will only be made worse.

A BETTER GOLF TO SWING

When you're slicing the ball the decision to use stiff shafts will not help, (even though they can negate a hook).

You need some help from the flexing of the shaft to aid in the squaring the of the club face.

Once you are using a shaft that is matched to your swing speed the focus should be given to technique.

Remember, an in to out swing path will not fix a slice. You need to have the club face squaring up first before working on the swing path.

K.I.S.S

Always use a flex of shaft that is compatible with your swing speed - Speak with your pro - have your swing speed measured.

25 THE TIP: HIT THE BALL WITH A CLOSED CLUB FACE TO PRODUCE A DRAW

WHY IS THIS TIP GIVEN?

Slicing the ball is a common problem with average golfers, therefore the draw is regarded as the holy grail of shot making.

A club face pointing left (closed) of the target at impact will produce a shot that curves to the left.

However, to produce a pure, safe and repeatable draw, you need to hit the ball with a slightly open clubface.

THE PROBLEM WITH IMPLEMENTING THE TIP

A club face that points left of the target at impact (closed) will cause the ball to curve from right to left and miss the target.

With the club face closed you must swing the club exactly parallel to the target line in order to hit the draw.

If you have the swing path a little left of the target (and a closed club face), you will hit a pull hook.

If you have the club path in to out, (with the club face closed), you get a loopy in to out hook.

Either way, the closed club face is a risky way to achieve a manageable draw.

A BETTER GOLF SWING

It might seem odd, but having an open club face to hit a draw will produce a soft landing *and* highly repeatable shot.

At the moment of impact, in relation to the ball target line, the club face needs to be a little open and pointing slightly right of the target.

The key to hitting a soft and consistent draw is to swing the club with an in to out swing path.

Even though the club face is open in relation to the *ball target line*, it will be slightly closed in relation to the *in to out swing path*.

With a slightly open club face striking the ball in relation to the target line (that's closed in relation to the swing path of the club head), the ball will have slight counter clockwise spin.

The ball will start a fraction right of the target, reach its highest point (the apex of the shot) and then drift back gently towards the target.

This is the best way to hit a repeatable classic draw.

K.I.S.S

Swing in to out with a slightly open clubface.

26 THE TIP: USE A DIFFERENT BALL POSITION FOR DIFFERENT CLUBS

WHY IS THE TIP GIVEN?

Obviously hitting a 9 iron off the ground and hitting a driver off the tee requires a different "angle of attack" throughout the hitting zone.

When using a short iron, play the ball back in the stance. That way we can hit down on the ball and take a pivot, while moving the ball way up to our left heel using a driver. This allows us to "sweep" the ball off the tee.

THE PROBLEM WITH IMPLEMENTING THE TIP

If you ask the vast majority of normal golfers what they would like to improve most with, it would most certainly be consistency.

If the point of contact and placement of the ball changes with each shot, (depending on what number club you are using), consistency of your swing will be greatly affected.

You will need to release the club early with a short iron if you are playing the ball back in the stance, and delay the release when playing the ball forward with the driver.

Either way, the consistency of your swing will suffer.

A BETTER GOLF SWING

A way to simplify your swing and improve consistency is to play the ball from the same point in your stance with all clubs.

As a general rule, most players will find that the best spot for the ball is just back from a line, drawn down from your left armpit. To change the "angle of attack" with different clubs, don't alter the ball position. Instead, you should be altering your weight distribution and stance width at address.

When playing a short iron, start with more weight on your front foot and a relatively narrow stance. With short irons you may want to experiment with keeping the weight on the front foot throughout the entire the swing.

This forward weight distribution will have you striking down and through the ball.

At the other end of the scale when you grab your driver, widen out your stance to at least shoulder width with more weight on your back foot. This will set you up for a more ascending blow.

The beauty of addressing the ball this way is that the point of contact will be the same with each club.

Your release pattern through the impact zone will be identical no matter what club you are playing, improving confidence and consistency.

K.I.S.S

Find your best ball position and then use it for all your clubs.

27 THE TIP: USE THE INTERLOCK OR OVERLAP GRIP

WHY IS THE TIP GIVEN?

Even though we have both of our hands on the club, it is good to have them working as one unit.

It makes sense to try and "marry" the hands together as much as possible. Intertwine your left index finger and right pinky, or lay the pinky of the right hand into the groove created between the index finger and the middle finger of the left hand.

THE PROBLEM WITH IMPLEMENTING THE TIP

The interlocking grip isn't a problem; it's *how you actually take this style of grip that matters.*

When a player is concentrating on linking their fingers, invariably the bottom hand (the right hand) will come to the grip from the *underside* of the club.

Once the bottom hand links from "underneath", it is much harder to get the palm of the right hand to wrap over and cover the left thumb.

The bottom hand ends up being placed into a strong position on the club. The right hand is therefore turned well to the right on the club, which will cause problems.

A BETTER GOLF SWING

These interlocking and overlapping grips are the overwhelming choice amongst the pros, because both of these styles do a good job of uniting the hands together.

However, more attention needs to be placed on the palm alignment and thumb location.

Once you hold the club with the top hand, make sure you bring the bottom hand (right hand) towards the grip from in front of the club. Cover the left thumb, which should be slightly offset to the right of the centre point of the grip, with the palm of the right hand.

This will allow the thumb of the right hand to be slightly offset to the left of the grip.

When viewing the grip from the front, the left thumb will be totally obscured by the right hand. Only at this point, should you focus on how the fingers at the "back" of the grip intertwine.

Concentrating on the "front" portion of the grip first and then the "back" portion, makes it easier to correctly align your hands.

K.I.S.S

Bring your hands together from the front and then intertwine.

28 THE TIP: SWING SLOWLY TO GAIN CONTROL OF YOUR SHOTS (AND SWING)

WHY IS THIS TIP GIVEN?

Slowing our swing down and focusing on hitting the ball softer supposedly corrects errors.

This slow swing reduces the strike power and any side spin applied to the ball.

This is suggested to straighten the shot pattern.

THE PROBLEM WITH IMPLEMENTING THE TIP

If you slow your swing to correct mistakes, you will just make *slow mistakes*.

If the ball is struck with an open club face and slow spin, this will produce a left to right side spin.

However, this slower swing will fail to fix the open club face.

A BETTER GOLF SWING

In order to control the ball, you must learn how "cause and effect" apply to the golf swing.

If you are slicing your shots, you need to ask yourself why the club face is open as it strikes the ball. When it comes to the speed of your swing, never alter the tempo of your swing to compensate for technical errors.

The appropriate speed at which you swing on full shots in golf could be compared to a second serve in tennis. You are not going to try and smash your first drive (because in golf we don't get to call fault) but you are not going to steer the ball either by swinging very slowly.

You should make a positive swing with enough speed and power for a complete and balanced follow through to be achieved.

K.I.S.S

Swing positive to a fully balanced follow through.

29 THE TIP: TAKE THE PUTTER STRAIGHT BACK AND STRAIGHT THROUGH.

WHY IS THIS TIP GIVEN?

Some might think that swinging the putter head on a straight line back and through will produce a putt that rolls straight towards your target.

THE PROBLEM WITH IMPLEMENTING THE TIP

Because a golfer stands to the side of the intended line of a putt, if you attempt to swing the putter straight back you will need use your hands to get the club head onto the straight line.

Once on this straight line on the backswing, the tendency is to swing the putter head across the ball on the forward swing and pull the putt.

A BETTER GOLF SWING

On almost all golf shots, except bunker or lob shots, you should swing the club back on an arc, and then back again through that same arc.

The putting stroke is no different. On the backswing, allow the putter head to naturally arc to the inside of the intended line. Swing back through on the same arc until you strike the ball.

Have the putter head follow the intended line of the putt only once you hit the ball.

You may need to manipulate the putter head to do this; however it has been shown (using super slow motion cameras) that top players prefer this inside to down the line putting stroke.

K.I.S.S

Inside on the backswing, inside on the downswing, down the line after impact.

30 THE TIP: REACH FOR THE SKY ON THE BACKSWING (AND EXTEND YOUR ARMS TOWARDS THE TARGET ON THE FORWARD SWING)

WHY IS THE TIP GIVEN?

A wide swing arc (the circle the club head makes from the start to finish of the swing) has long been regarded as a major power source and distance generator.

To achieve a wide swing arc, players are encouraged to "reach for the sky" on the backswing and throw the arms towards the target after impact.

THE PROBLEM WITH IMPLEMENTING THE TIP

The best power source of a swing is the coiling and uncoiling of the torso.

As soon as your arms are "reaching for the sky" and "throwing towards the target", they will be moving away from the power source of the swing (your torso).

Reaching for the sky on the backswing can cause your arms to end in an overly upright position, which damages your swing. Even though it feels like there is a lot of power with the arms swinging away from the body, the opposite is actually true.

The arms won't be travelling as fast as they could have been, due to the torso and arms becoming disconnected.

A BETTER GOLF SWING

Instead, at the top of the backswing, concentrate on the position of your right arm.

Make sure the upper arm is parallel to the ground when flexing at 90 degrees or less.

This is as "high" as the right arm can be while keeping the left arm "on plane".

After striking the ball, resist the pulling motion on your arms that is caused by the weight of the club head.

By resisting the feeling that the arms are flinging out towards the target, you will have the arms working and turning with the power source of your swing (the unwinding torso).

This is a great way to achieve consistency and generate power.

K.I.S.S

Right arm parallel at the top - keep the arms connected to the body through impact.

CONCLUSION

You now have a whole new way to look at some of the oldest and most common golfing tips.

Your golfing buddies may resist these new ideas, but this only shows how ingrained certain golfing tips have become.

Have faith, and know that by learning **a better golf swing** you will achieve all the positive results that the original tips promised, but in a more reliable, safe and consistent fashion.

Good luck and good golfing!

Damien.

P.S. – If you feel like you have picked up **any bit of advice or tip that is going to improve the quality and your enjoyment of the game**, I would love it if you could leave a review of this book.

I've always loved the game of golf and I've always loved trying to help others with their game where I can. Thanks again.

DISCLAIMER

The following ebook is reproduced below with the goal of providing information that is as accurate and reliable as possible. Regardless, purchasing this ebook can be seen as consent to the fact that the publisher and the author of this book are in no way experts on the topic discussed within and that any recommendations or suggestions that are made herein are for entertainment purposes only. Professionals should be consulted as needed prior to undertaking any of the action endorsed herein.

This declaration is deemed fair and valid by both the American Bar Association and the Committee of Publishers Association and is legally binding throughout the United States.

Furthermore, the transmission, duplication or reproduction of any of the following work including specific information will be considered an illegal act irrespective of if it is done electronically or in print. This extends to creating secondary or tertiary copy of the work or a recorded copy and is only allowed with express written consent from the publisher. All additional rights reserved.

The information in the following pages is broadly considered to be a truthful and accurate account of facts and as such any inattention, use or misuse of the information in question by the reader will render any resulting action solely under their purview. There are no scenarios in which the publisher or the original author of this work can be in any fashion deemed liable for any hardship or damages that may befall after undertaking information described herein.

Additionally, the information in the following pages is intended only for informational purposes and should thus be thought of as universal. As befitting in nature, it is presented without assurance regarding its prolonged validity or interim quality. Trademarks that are mentioned are done without written consent and can in no way be considered an endorsement from the trademark holder.

45757140R00040

Printed in Poland
by Amazon Fulfillment
Poland Sp. z o.o., Wrocław